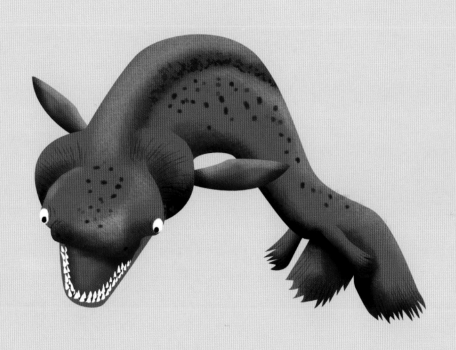

Author:

Alex Woolf studied history at Essex University, England. He is the author of over 60 books for children, including *The Science of Acne and Warts: The Itchy Truth About Skin, You Wouldn't Want to Live Without Bees!,* and *You Wouldn't Want to Live Without Vegetables!*

Series creator:

David Salariya was born in Dundee, Scotland. He has illustrated a wide range of books and has created and designed many new series for publishers in the UK and overseas. David established The Salariya Book Company in 1989. He lives in Brighton, England, with his wife, illustrator Shirley Willis, and their son, Jonathan.

Artists:

Andy Rowland
Bryan Beach

Editor:

Jacqueline Ford

© The Salariya Book Company Ltd MMXVIII
No part of this publication may be reproduced in whole or in part, or stored in a retrieval system, or transmitted in any form or by any means, electronic, mechanical, photocopying, recording, or otherwise, without written permission of the publisher. For information regarding permission, write to the copyright holder.

Published in Great Britain in 2018 by
The Salariya Book Company Ltd
25 Marlborough Place, Brighton BN1 1UB

ISBN-13: 978-0-531-25832-3 (lib. bdg.) 978-0-531-26902-2 (pbk.)

A CIP catalog record for this book is available
from the Library of Congress.

Printed and bound in China.
Printed on paper from sustainable sources.
1 2 3 4 5 6 7 8 9 10 R 27 26 25 24 23 22 21 20 19 18

PAPER FROM
SUSTAINABLE
FORESTS

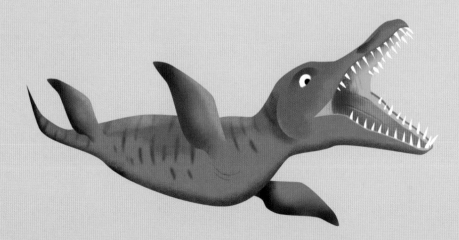

The Science of Sea Monsters

Prehistoric Reptiles of the Sea

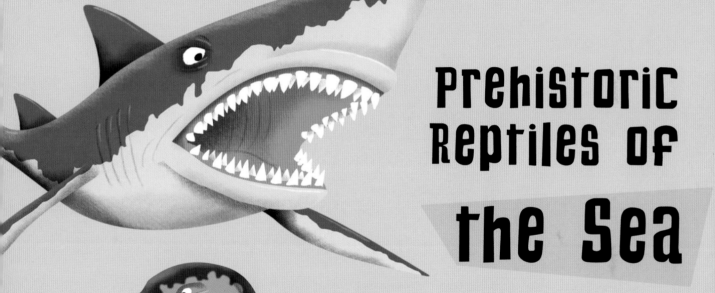

written by
Alex Woolf

Illustrated by
Andy Rowland

Franklin Watts®
An Imprint of Scholastic Inc.

Contents

Cameroceras

Dunkleosteus

| Silurian: 444-419 mya | Devonian: 419-359 mya | Carboniferous: 359-299 mya | Permian: 299-252 mya |

Mya = Million years ago

Introduction

Millions of years ago, the oceans teemed with creatures that were every bit as fascinating and ferocious as the dinosaurs that ruled the land. Some of them we would recognize today, like turtles, sharks, and crocodiles—except back then they tended to be a lot bigger! There were also sea serpents, fanged fish, and squid-like tentacled creatures that weren't very different from their modern equivalents. And then there were the marine reptiles that seem completely alien to our modern eyes. These included the massive-jawed pliosaur, the super speedy mosasaur, and the long-necked plesiosaur.

This book covers a very long period, from 430 million to just 1.6 million years ago, and not all these species existed at the same time—yet many were the dominant predators of their era. Read on to discover how these awesome creatures lived, how they hunted, and how we know about them today.

Nothosaurus

Mosasaurs

Triassic: 252–201 mya	Jurassic: 201–145 mya	Cretaceous: 145–65 mya

Flippers and Tails

During the Triassic Period, some land reptiles began venturing into the sea to feed on fish. Over millions of years, their bodies adapted to a watery lifestyle. Their bodies became more streamlined, their tails became more developed, and their legs became paddle-like flippers.

Unlike the smaller, gentler turtles of today, Archelon was a fierce predator. It was 13 feet (4 meters) long, weighed 2.2 tons (2 metric tons) and could crush a squid with one bite of its massive beak.

Killer Features

Prehistoric ocean predators developed a number of killer features to make them fast, deadly in attack, and strong in defense. For attack, they evolved weapons such as tentacles, beaks, jaws, and sharp teeth. For speed, they evolved fins and tails, along with powerful muscles to drive them. Slower creatures needed other survival methods, such as the thick, protective shell of the Archelon, a prehistoric kind of turtle; or the tough plating of the Dunkleosteus, a predatory fish.

You're so slow!

I'm also tough to eat!

Teeth

Prehistoric marine predators evolved different kinds of teeth to suit their hunting needs. Kronosaurus had long, conical teeth with smooth sides, so it may have hunted by spearing small prey and swallowing them whole. Dakosaurus had serrated teeth, so it could attack larger prey, and chomp their flesh into smaller, digestible chunks.

Don't want to get my teeth stuck in anything too big.

Claws

Arthropods, the ancestors of today's spiders, insects, and lobsters, evolved claws as a hunting tool. One of the earliest known was *Yawunik kootenayi*, which prowled the oceans 500 million years ago. The lobsterlike creature had six claws. Four of the claws had teeth!

Claws with teeth? Now that's overkill!

Some marine predators evolved a method of hunting called suction feeding. By opening their jaws very quickly, they caused a sucking pressure that pulled prey into their mouths.

Fascinating Fact

Various marine creatures evolved tentacles as sensing organs or to move themselves around. The prehistoric giant squid Haboroteuthis also evolved them for hunting. Like today's squid, Haboroteuthis probably had a pair of long tentacles for capturing prey, and four shorter pairs, equipped with suckers, for holding the victim and pulling it into the squid's mouth.

Terrifying Tentacles

Tentacles and Beak

Mmm, a crunchy one!

Cameroceras had excellent eyesight, so it could track movement even in very dark waters. When a fish or mollusk came close, it would grab it and pull it toward its beak-like mouth. The beak was strong enough to bite right through the hardest shells and exoskeletons.

L urking in the depths of the ocean some 430 million years ago was a massive squid-like monster called the Cameroceras. This tentacled titan may have been up to 30 feet (9 m) in length, making it the largest mollusk ever known. Cameroceras probably hunted by lying on the seabed and waiting for its prey to pass within reach. Its long tentacles grew from the base of its head, similar to modern cuttlefish. The tentacles had sticky hooks, which it used to trap its prey. Inside its beak was a "toothed" tongue called a radula, which it used to scrape out the soft tissue in its prey's shell.

I just stay very still and my food comes to me!

Chambered Shell

The shell of Cameroceras was like a long horn made up of separate chambers (its name means "chambered shell"). The mantle, or main body, of the creature lay in the outermost chamber, closest to the opening. As it grew, the shell grew to accommodate it.

Descendants

Cameroceras was a cephalopod, part of the class that includes octopuses, squid, and cuttlefish. Studying these animals gives us clues about the appearance and behavior of their awesome ancestor, even though all we have left of it is part of its shell.

I'm proud we're related.

If it wanted to rise, Cameroceras could pump fluid out of the inner chambers of its shell to give it buoyancy.

Cameroceras was able to stay horizontal because the end tip of its shell was heavy enough to balance the weight of its body.

Famous Fossil Finds

Prehistoric squid fossils are rare, because these creatures were mostly soft tissue. So it was a surprise in 2015 when a team led by Kazushige Tanabe found the beak of a prehistoric giant squid-like creature in 80-million-year-old rock near Hokkaido, Japan. The previously unknown species was named Haboroteuthis.

Suction Jaws

Dunkleosteus had complex movable joints within its skull that allowed it to open its jaws in just ½₀ of a second. This was quick enough to create a suction effect, pulling prey into its mouth. It then closed its jaws with a bite force estimated at 1,650 pounds (750 kilograms)—enough to slice through even the most well-armored prey.

Help! I can't escape!

Although Dunkleosteus was a powerful swimmer, the weight of its armor probably made it very slow, so it may have ambushed rather than chased its prey. Its sucking jaws meant it didn't have to catch its food; it just had to get close enough and open its mouth.

Ferocious Fish

In Devonian times, around 370 million years ago, the dominant ocean predator was a gigantic horror fish. At up to 33 feet (10 m) in length, Dunkleosteus was the biggest animal on the planet in its day, and would remain so until the arrival of the dinosaurs. Its enormous body was armored with tough plating. Instead of teeth, Dunkleosteus possessed a pair of sharp, bony plates that were actually extensions of its jaw. These, combined with powerful jaw muscles, could crack shells, snap bones, and slice through flesh.

No one messes with me!

Indigestion

Dunkleosteus's sucking jaws dragged in anything close by. As a result, the giant fish appears to have suffered from indigestion. Its fossils are often found with the regurgitated, semi-digested remains of fish it had eaten and then later thrown up.

Ugh! I ate too much again!

Cannibals?

Paleontologists have found unhealed bite marks on Dunkleosteus armor. This strongly suggests that these creatures ate each other, perhaps when other food was hard to find.

Hey, sorry! It's a fish-eat-fish world!

Paleontologists aren't exactly sure what the rear part of Dunkleosteus looked like, because only the armored front part has been preserved. Reconstructions of the back of the fish are based on smaller fish from the same family.

Fascinating Fact

Dunkleosteus was not the only giant predatory fish of the Devonian. Another was Titanichthys, which could also grow up to 33 feet (10 m) long. But this gentle, blunt-jawed creature probably ate by swimming open-mouthed through schools of small fish, or maybe it filtered for krill, making it one of the earliest known filter feeders.

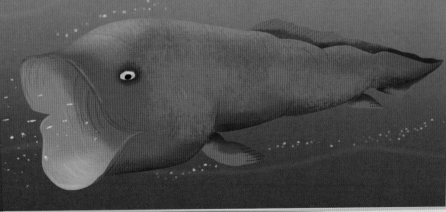

Web-Footed Wonders

Nothosaurus was a sleek, aggressive predator of the Triassic Period. Up to 13 feet (4 m) long, with paddle-like limbs, a long snout, and powerful tail, it looked a little like a huge modern seal. Like seals, it basked on land and hunted in the water, using its webbed fingers and toes to move around. Nothosaurus had sharp, outward-pointing teeth, ideal for trapping wriggling, slippery fish or squid.

Hunting

Nothosaurus used its tail, legs, and webbed feet to push and steer itself through the water in an undulating motion. It was an ambush predator, sneaking up on schools of fish, then putting on a burst of speed. Once trapped in its powerful jaws, few animals could escape.

Enough basking! Go catch some fish!

Cute Cousin

Nothosaurus had several close relatives within the "nothosaur" family. One of the smallest of these was Lariosaurus, some just 24 inches (60 centimeters) long.

Lariosaurus had tiny flippers and was not a great swimmer, so probably spent lots of time on dry land or in the shallows. Surprisingly, its back toes were not webbed.

Sleek Swimmer

The nothosaurs would eventually evolve into the plesiosaurs. One nothosaur that closely resembled the plesiosaurs was Ceresiosaurus. Reaching 10 feet (3 m) in length, it had a long neck and tail and fully developed flippers, with no trace of webbed toes, making it well adapted to aquatic life.

If you hurt me, I'll tell my big cousin!

Many experts believe Lariosaurus did not lay eggs but instead gave birth to live young.

Survival Tactics

The Nothosaurus would stay in sight of land when swimming, in case of potential attacks from an ichthyosaur or a shark. When on land, it would keep close to the shore, to avoid being preyed upon by a hungry archosaur.

Strange Fish

I'm not what you'd call a picky eater.

One of the strangest-looking ichthyosaurs was Shonisaurus. It had a small head, a huge, round body, and its only teeth were at the tips of its jaws. Shonisaurus may have gathered food simply by swimming forward with a wide open mouth.

The biggest of all the ichthyosaurs, and the biggest marine predator of all time, was Shastasaurus, estimated to have been 68 feet (21 m) in length.

Long-Nosed Lizard Fish

Over 250 million years ago, in the Triassic Period, there appeared a species of marine animal that resembled a scary dolphin. The ichthyosaurs ("fish lizards") thrived in the world's oceans for 160 million years. There were many varieties, ranging from 12-inch (30 cm) minnows to 68-foot (21 m) beasts. Although they evolved from land-based reptiles, the ichthyosaurs had streamlined bodies, well adapted to the ocean. Along with dolphin-like jaws filled with sharp teeth, they had crescent-shaped tails, giving them impressive speed through the water.

We may look like dolphins, but we're not friendly!

Big Eyes

Thanks to their large eyes, ichthyosaurs could hunt at night and at great depths. One species, Temnodontosaurus, had eyes with a 10-inch (25 cm) diameter, rivaling those of giant squid. This would have allowed it to see at a depth of up to 5,250 feet (1,600 m).

What big eyes you have!

All the better to see you with!

Ichthyo-Sword

En garde!

One species of icthyosaur looked like a swordfish, with a long, thin upper jaw. It was named Excalibosaurus, after King Arthur's legendary sword. It might have used its sword to probe for food on the ocean floor, as a weapon in battles, or to kill its prey.

With a cruising speed of up to 22 miles (35 kilometers) per hour, ichthyosaurs could chase down even the fastest of prey. Thalattoarchon, a giant early species, had big bladelike teeth for killing prey its own size.

Can You Believe It?

In 2011, two geologists in Nevada found a set of nine Shonisaurus fossils mysteriously arranged in a pattern resembling an octopus. They proposed it was a "work of art" by a prehistoric giant octopus with advanced intelligence. The idea was dismissed by the scientific community, and the mystery remains unsolved.

Snake-Necked Swimmers

Elasmosaurus swam slowly in a wavelike motion. It used its front flippers for steering and its rear flippers for propelling itself through the water.

Teeth

Long, thin teeth protruded from the mouth of Elasmosaurus. The teeth meshed together, trapping fish securely when Elasmosaurus bit them. The teeth were designed for trapping rather than chewing, so fish were swallowed whole.

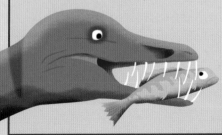

P lesiosaurs were a family of long-necked marine reptiles that roamed the oceans from around 220 million to 65 million years ago. Among the most remarkable plesiosaurs was Elasmosaurus. It had one of the longest necks of any plesiosaur, extending up to 23 feet (7 m). With its 72 vertebrae, the neck had a snakelike flexibility. Elasmosaurus could swim beneath a school of fish, hiding its body in the depths, then use its long, agile neck to dart its head into the school and snap up a mouthful of them.

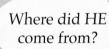

Where did HE come from?

Swimming

Elasmosaurus didn't have gills, so it would have had to surface occasionally for air. With its huge lungs, it could probably survive on a single breath for up to 20 minutes.

Lucky you! I have to go up to breathe.

Swallowing Stones

We know Elasmosaurus swallowed stones because they have been found in fossils. The stones (known as gastroliths) may have helped with digestion. As Elasmosaurus moved, the stones ground together in its stomach, helping to soften the food.

Uh-oh! I need to eat more stones!

Because of its enormous size and the weight of its neck, Elasmosaurus would not have been able to raise more than its head out of the water.

Fascinating Fact

When Elasmosaurus was discovered in 1868, paleontologist Edward Drinker Cope had never seen such a creature before and he assembled an animal with a short neck and a long tail. Later, when he realized his error, he placed the head at the correct end.

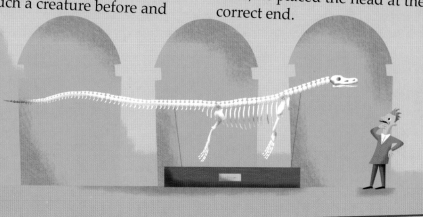

T. rex of the Sea

Liopleurodon's jaws were huge, and it had a bite powerful enough to keep a grip on a huge, struggling Ichthyosaurus. Some of its teeth were 8 inches (20 cm) in length, the size of *T. rex*'s teeth. The teeth stuck out in front to form a vicious trap for its prey.

In 2006, paleontologists unearthed two massive pliosaur skeletons in Norway. After six years of study, they announced these as a new pliosaur species, the Pliosaur funkei. It was 39 feet (12 m) long, with a 6.5-foot (2 m) skull, and a bite four times as powerful as T. rex!

Giant Jaws

Pliosaurs were relatives of the plesiosaurs with extra-long heads and short necks. Among the most fearsome was Liopleurodon, which lived around 160 million years ago. This monster could grow to over 20 feet (6 m), and one-fifth of its length was taken up by its skull and jaws! It must have been a ferocious hunter and the apex predator of its time. As evidence of this, half-eaten ichthyosaurs and squid have been found in its fossilized remains, and its teeth have scarred the flippers of plesiosaurs.

Just call me Jaws— it's easier to say!

Speed

Like all plesiosaurs, Liopleurodon had four flippers. The broad, flat, paddle-like shape of these flippers meant the reptile could propel itself through the water at high speed, and was able to accelerate to catch its prey.

Speed up! This is too easy!

The first evidence of Liopleurodon was three teeth dug up in France in 1873—in fact, Liopleurodon means "smooth-sided teeth." Why was it found in France? Because when Liopleurodon was alive, most of western Europe was covered by a shallow sea.

Smell Sense

Studies of Liopleurodon's skull have shown it had an excellent sense of smell. By funneling water through its forward-facing nostrils, it could pick up trace chemicals secreted by its prey long before it could see it, much as sharks do today.

Hmmm… I smell dinner!

Famous Fossil Finds

In 1985, the fossil of a giant pliosaur was discovered by a university student in Aramberri, Mexico. Experts wrongly identified it as a Liopleurodon with an estimated length of 49 feet (15 m).

Whatever it is, the "Monster of Aramberri" is possibly the largest pliosaur ever discovered, and continues to fascinate paleontologists to this day.

Built for Speed

Mosasaurs were quick! They moved like sharks, with broad tails that swept from side to side to give them locomotive power. Their bodies were streamlined and covered in smooth scales to help them slip rapidly through the water.

Fearsomely Fast

Sleeker and faster than pliosaurs, mosasaurs were the undisputed apex predators of Late Cretaceous waters. There were many varieties, ranging from the 3-foot-long (1 m) Dallasaurus to the 50-foot (15 m) monster, Tylosaurus, and their fossils have been found on almost every continent. They were especially well adapted to warm, shallow, inland seas, and occasionally rivers. Mosasaurs were air-breathing reptiles that were descended from land-based lizards. In fact, their flippers were composed of webbed finger and toe bones.

The mosasaur Dallasaurus was amphibious (capable of swimming in shallow waters), but it also had fingers and claws that allowed it to move around on land.

Race you for it!

Don't even bother!

Trash Cans of the Sea

Mosasaurs had voracious appetites and would eat virtually anything. Their stomach contents have been found to include ammonites, bony fish, sea turtles, plesiosaurs, sharks, other mosasaurs, and even seabirds. Some mosasaurs, like Globidens, had blunt spherical teeth for crushing mollusk shells.

Shall I?... Oh, why not!

Snake Jaws

Like their distant ancestors, snakes, mosasaurs had two sets of teeth in their upper jaws. The second, set farther back, enabled them to hold on to struggling prey. Also like snakes, mosasaurs had double-hinged jaws and flexible skulls, so they could expand their mouths to fit large prey!

You couldn't eat me.

Wanna bet?

Mosasaurs were probably countershaded, meaning they had dark backs and light underbellies, like great white sharks. We know this because in 2014 researchers found the pigment melanin in the fossilized scales of a mosasaur.

Famous Fossil Finds

The 1764 discovery of Mosasaurus, the original mosasaur, by quarry workers near Maastricht, Holland, was hugely significant. They were the first fossilized remains to be identified as belonging to an ancient creature. It made scientists realize that species could become extinct, and that Earth had been populated by strange-looking animals since long before Biblical times.

Sarcosuchus had a bulbous tip called a bulla at the end of its snout. Scientists don't know what this was for, but it may have helped Sarcosuchus make sounds or improved its sense of smell.

How Big Were They?

Hmm, this one must have been around 36 feet (11 m).

Paleontologists have used fossil remains of skulls, teeth, and other body parts to estimate the size and weight of these creatures. The biggest Deinosuchus was probably about 40 feet (12 m) and weighed 9.3 tons (8.5 MT). Its skull alone was longer than an adult human is tall. The biggest known Sarcosuchus was around 38 feet (11.6 m).

Killer Crocs

With their enormous jaws, sharp teeth, and scaly bodies, crocodiles seem to have crawled straight out of the Age of the Dinosaurs. In a way they have, because the first ones appeared on Earth some 200 million years ago. But the crocodiles we see today are gentle compared to the monster crocs of the Cretaceous. Among the very biggest were Deinosuchus ("terrible crocodile") and Sarcosuchus ("flesh crocodile"). These prehistoric crocs ate fish, turtles, dead animals, and even large dinosaurs.

Surprise!

Death Roll

Deinosuchus ambushed dinosaurs and other land animals at the water's edge, then dragged them into the water. With its prey held firmly in its jaws, it turned over and over in a "death roll" until the creature was dead.

Deadly Bite

The huge jaws of Deinosuchus contained at least 44 teeth. Those at the front were sharp for trapping prey and tearing at flesh. The ones at the back were rounded and blunt for crushing. The animal's bite force has been estimated at 2 to 10 tons (1.8 to 9 MT), greater than a *T. rex*'s, enabling it to crush the shell of a turtle.

Study of the growth rings in Sarcosuchus suggest it could live 50 to 60 years, compared to a range from about 20 years or less to the life span of a human, depending on the species.

Fascinating Fact

Deinosuchus bite marks have been found in the fossils of the mighty carnivores Albertosaurus and Appalachiosaurus (a species of tyrannosaur). This shows that Deinosuchus was willing to take on even the biggest and fiercest dinosaurs of its day.

I got this fighting a crocodile.

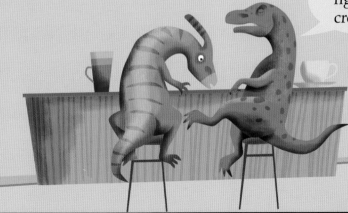

Bite Force

Megalodon had the most powerful bite of any creature that's ever lived. While a great white shark bites with 1.9 tons (1.8 MT) of force, Megalodon clamped its jaws down on its prey with a force of 12 to 20 tons (10.8 to 18.2 MT)—enough to crush the skull of a whale or shatter the shell of a giant turtle.

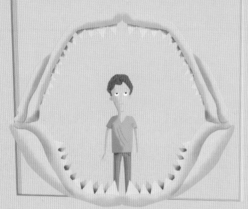

Super Shark

The greatest marine predator of all time was a shark. But this was like no shark living before or since. This was Megalodon. From nose to tail, it measured a monstrous 56 feet (17 m)—that's three times longer than today's great white shark—and it weighed up to 83 tons (75 MT). Megalodon, meaning "giant tooth," was well named, because its teeth were a whopping 7 inches (17 cm) long. It ruled the oceans from 16 million to 2.6 million years ago—into the time of early humans.

All that remains of Megalodon are teeth and spinal fragments called centra. These contain growth rings, like trees. By studying the rings, paleontologists can figure out a Megalodon's growth rate and its age at death.

The only thing I'm scared of is another Megalodon!

 Megalodon may have evolved from an earlier giant shark, Odotus, which lived 40 million to 60 million years ago and grew to 29 feet (9 m).

Extinction

Though some people fear Megalodon still lurks in the ocean depths, scientists are convinced it's extinct. Why did it die out? One reason could be that the giant shark was unable to adapt to the cooler conditions of the last ice age.

Brrrr!

Hunting Style

To judge from attack marks on Megalodon's victims, it was an extremely aggressive predator. Unlike the great white, which attacks its prey's soft underbelly, Megalodon targeted the skull, spine, ribs, and flippers. With such powerful jaws, it could bite through bone to get to the flesh beneath.

Fascinating Fact

Megalodon teeth have been discovered all over the world since ancient times. They were believed to be rocks fallen from the moon, or tongues of dragons and giant serpents. It was Danish scientist Nicolas Steno who, in 1666, correctly identified them as shark's teeth. He realized they'd turned to stone (fossilized), and for this discovery he is known as the father of paleontology.

Livyatan was an apex predator, and is likely to have preyed on sharks, baleen whales, seals, dolphins, porpoises, turtles, and other large marine animals.

Leviathan

In November 2008, paleontologist Klaas Post was working in the coastal desert of Peru when he chanced upon a truly extraordinary find. It was a 10-foot (3 m) skull of an enormous, extinct whale that lived 12 million to 13 million years ago. Klaas and his team named it Livyatan (Hebrew for Leviathan). They estimated it was 44 to 57 feet (13.5 to 17.5 m) long, roughly the size of a modern sperm whale. But unlike the sperm whale, Livyatan had huge teeth. The biggest of these was over 14 inches (36 cm)—the size of an elephant tusk, and bigger than any animal tooth ever found.

Brutal Bite

Livyatan had huge jaw-closing muscles, and its short, wide snout allowed it to bite down powerfully with its front teeth. The teeth were deeply embedded in the jawbone, so were unlikely to break off. They were interlocked for a flesh-piercing bite, and angled forward to give Livyatan a better grip on its prey.

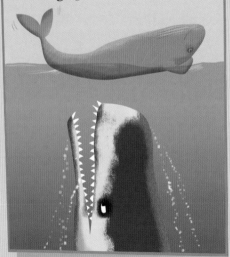

Livyatan Versus Megalodon?

Livyatan lived at the same time as the monster shark Megalodon, and they may even have fought each other. As a warm-blooded mammal, Livyatan had a bigger brain, so it may have been quicker to react in a fight. However, it wasn't the speediest of animals, and its huge bulk would have offered a tempting target for the shark.

This could be the biggest fight since the Cretaceous!

Skull Mystery

Livyatan, like the sperm whale, had an organ inside its head called the spermaceti. The sperm whale uses it to control its buoyancy when it dives for squid. But Livyatan probably wasn't a deep diver, so why did it need it? It may have been for echolocation or to head-butt other males in mating contests.

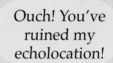

Ouch! You've ruined my echolocation!

The whale's full name is Livyatan melvillei, named after Herman Melville, author of Moby-Dick, a famous novel about a man's hunt for a whale.

Can You Believe It?

In 2016, a gigantic tooth was discovered in Beaumaris Bay, Australia. The tooth belonged to an extinct species of sperm whale that may have been a species of Livyatan. The tooth is 5 million to 6 million years old, which suggests that Livyatan, or something like it, was alive a lot more recently than experts originally believed.

Strange Sea Hunters

Circular Saw

Helicoprion was a very strange-looking shark: The teeth in its lower jaw were arranged in a spiral pattern, known as a tooth whorl. The tooth whorl may have been at the front of the jaw and used to saw through the shells of ammonites; or it may have been farther back, suggesting a diet of soft-bodied creatures.

A giant claw of the sea scorpion Jaekelopterus was unearthed in a German quarry in 2007.

As we've seen, the prehistoric ocean was full of awesome predators, each with their own particular method of hunting prey. Here, we look at some of the more unusual prehistoric predators, who evolved their own fascinating hunting techniques. Some of them were terrifying—like Jaekelopterus, for example. This sea scorpion was 8 feet (2.5 m) long—the biggest arthropod ever. It lurked in swamps, pouncing on passing animals with its vicious 18-inch (46 cm) spiked claws. The only good news is that it lived 390 million years ago!

BOO!

Saber-Toothed Herring

Enchodus was a seemingly modest fish of the Late Cretaceous that looked a little like a modern herring—except for its mouth full of vicious, sharp teeth. Enchodus had two huge fangs at the front of its mouth that could grow up to 2.4 inches (6 cm) long. A school of these piranha-like predators could make quick work of much larger marine creatures.

Let me bite first!

No, me!

Sting in the Tail

Not all prehistoric marine monsters died out. One that's still with us is the giant freshwater stingray, which first evolved 100 million years ago. It can reach up to 10 feet (3 m) in width, and to add to the horror, it has a 15-inch (38 cm) barbed poison spike in its rear that can pierce bone!

Yup, I'm still here I'm afraid.

What was the purpose of the Helicoprion's tooth whorl? Was it used as a lash against fish, or a rasp for cutting shells? The debate continues.

Fascinating Fact

Another prehistoric predator still alive today is the frilled shark, known as the "living fossil" because it dates back at least 100 million years. This eel-like shark captures its prey by bending its flexible body and then lunging forward like a snake. It then traps its prey in jaws lined with hundreds of backward-facing needlelike teeth.

Frilled to meet you!

Glossary

Ammonite An extinct mollusk with a flat-coiled spiral shell.

Amphibious Adapted for living both on land and in water.

Apex predator A predator at the top of the food chain, upon which no other creatures prey.

Aquatic Relating to water.

Archosaur A reptile belonging to a large group that includes dinosaurs and crocodiles.

Arthropod An invertebrate animal from a group that includes insects, spiders, and crustaceans.

Bulbous Fat, round, or bulging.

Buoyancy The ability of something to float in water.

Carnivore A meat-eating animal.

Cephalopod A group of predatory mollusks that includes octopuses and squid.

Conical Cone shaped.

Cretaceous A period in Earth's history lasting from approximately 145 million to 65 million years ago.

Devonian A period in Earth's history lasting from approximately 419 million to 359 million years ago.

Echolocation The location of objects by means of reflected sound, as used by dolphins, whales, and bats.

Extinct No longer surviving.

Fossil The remains of a prehistoric organism embedded in rock and preserved in a petrified (stony) form.

Growth rings Rings in bone that show the life span of animals.

Ice age One of several episodes in Earth's history when temperatures fell and ice sheets spread across Earth's surface.

Invertebrate An animal without a backbone.

Krill Small, shrimplike crustaceans.

Locomotive (of an animal) Having the power of progressive motion.

Mammal A warm-blooded, vertebrate animal. Female mammals produce milk for their young and usually give birth to live young.

Marine Relating to or found in the sea.

Melanin A dark brown to black pigment.

Mollusk A group of invertebrate organisms, including snails, squid, and octopuses.

Organ A part of an organism that is self-contained and has a particular function.

Paleontologist An expert in fossil animals and plants.

Pigment A natural substance that creates color in animal or plant tissue.

Predator An animal that hunts and kills other animals.

Regurgitated Swallowed food that has been brought up again.

Reptile A cold-blooded vertebrate animal. Reptiles include snakes, lizards, and crocodiles.

Secreted Produced and discharged (a substance).

Serrated Having a jagged, sawlike edge.

Tentacle A slender, flexible limb of an animal, especially around the mouth of an invertebrate, used for grasping or moving around.

Titan Something of very great size and strength.

Triassic A period in Earth's history lasting from approximately 252 million to 201 million years ago.

Vertebrae The small bones that make up the backbone of an animal.

Vertebrate An animal with a backbone.

Voracious Wanting or devouring great quantities of food.

Warm-blooded Describing animals, such as mammals and birds, that maintain a constant body temperature.

Index